The Book Of Enlightenment

By S & C Enamorado

Copyright 2018 © By S & C Enamorado

ISBN: 978-1-9994435-0-4
E-ISBN: 978-1-9994435-1-1

First Edition, 2018

All rights reserved. No part of this publication may be reproduced, distributed, or transmitted in any form or by any means, including photocopying, recording, or other electronic or mechanical methods, without the prior written permission of the publisher. This book has a copyright in both Canada, and USA.

1bookofenlightenment@gmail.com

Table of Contents

I. ENLIGHTENMENT 1

II. THE UNIVERSE 14
    Creation 19
    Religion 25

III. ENERGY 32
    Ethereal Realm 39
    The Veil 41

IV. ENTITIES 47
    Destiny 51
    Fate 54
    Karma 56
    Karmic parasites 59
    Karmic balance 60

V. SOULS 63
Broken Souls & Broken Destinies 71
Past Lives 76
Free Will 80
The Afterlife 83
Heaven & Hell 86
Near-death Experiences 89

VI. THE SUPERNATURAL 92
Universal Messages 97
Meditation 102

VII. GREATER PURPOSE 107
Path To Enlightenment 113
Generation of Enlightenment 119

I.

ENLIGHTENMENT

Enlightenment, a term often used to refer to a spiritual awakening—a higher level of consciousness where one harbors an enhanced knowledge of the fundamental truths of existence. The Buddha was allegedly the first to attain this state of spiritual awareness. Despite questions remaining about his life, it is known his knowledge emerged as a result of deep meditation; focusing his mind, body, and spirit on what had been concealed within his own consciousness. Thus, he became the historical figure from which Buddhism originated. Though before he shared his wisdom, he was also a human being who followed a lifetime pertaining to a civilization and culture, which belongs to a certain time in history. He experienced the same emotions humanity encounters today and perceived all thoughts through his conscious mind, as everybody does. He only became Buddha as a result of his actions, intentions and motivations. His will to succeed was greater than any concern, skepticism or distractions. The point is: the knowledge needed to achieve enlightenment is already concealed within everyone's subconscious. If wholeheartedly desired, anyone can access and develop the awareness of their inner selves to challenge the concepts of life and find the spiritual answers they seek.

Countries, cultures and religions may divide the world but the fact remains that humanity relates and connects by other means; the bond we share originates from a much deeper part of the human self. Often mentioned as one's true self, the soul is the energy which contains the wisdom of existence. This information is constantly transmitted in various forms of energy to the mind. A soul guides a person throughout its lifetime, assisting with ethical decisions, providing inspiration, and challenging the mind's prejudice and preconception of reality. The human consciousness is only a fragment of who a being truly is. A conscious mind learns from its environment and stores memories of its past. It also develops behaviors as well as ideologies due to series of events and experiences which have occurred in its current lifetime. The subconscious, however, has reincarnated multiple times, allowed to see and experience other places in the universe. Someone's inner self can not be represented by a country, religion, social status, ethnicity, gender or sexuality. These are concepts of society established through mankind's history. Everyone is an individual being who perceives and experiences the world from a singular point of view, but we are all from the same race and we all originate from the same place.

Spirituality has been apart of every civilization throughout human history and is still embraced by multiple cultures today. There is a persistent belief in concepts such as spirit, karma and destiny despite any proof of authenticity because a soul already possesses the awareness of its existence. Humanity kept believing in these concepts because our inner selves are incapable of denying their spiritual origin. Through science, it is proven that energy cannot be destroyed or created but only transformed. The soul, which is in constant communication with the mind, transmits its energy in form of emotions, feelings, thoughts and intuition. The energy is then processed by the conscious and also transformed into other forms of energy which are released into the cosmos.

Most of today's religions, despite creating division all over the globe, have acknowledged a higher being or a divine spirit. Humanity has always longed for the truth about its existence because of the peculiarity of our species. There is a constant curiosity that enables mankind to search for answers. In the fields of science, this curiosity transforms into research and sometimes lead to new discoveries, new understandings or to an evolution of technologies. The soul is already aware that there is indeed a divine power; so the mind will yearn for a personal connection, a faith that feels like the right one or something that makes the most sense to the inner self.

Life is a cycle designed for souls to evolve in an imperfect world, to grow in different environments, to create an impact in society's evolution and to experience emotions such as love and compassion. Still, a single lifetime will not result in much growth, which is why life requires a soul to be born and reborn and reborn again until its evolution is complete; or, until the soul travels to the Afterlife. A soul must face recurring circumstances in order to observe if it will repeat previous mistakes. The conscious brain and the soul continuously exchange energy such as emotions or feelings when confronted by any situation. Consequently, when reborn and experiencing an equivalent situation, the soul, carrying some wisdom, instinctively guides the mind to the best outcome. A human mind is not meant to know more than what is learned in a specific lifetime because improvement would not be possible if the mind was aware of its soul's past experiences. Remembering other lives would be comparable to completing an exam, receiving the answers, and then completing the same exam again.

To be Enlightened does not mean to know who one was in a previous life; it means being aware of how the universe functions and how it connects with the self. Enlightenment gives the knowledge to face any obstacles or event from a more forgiving and less individualistic perspective. An Enlightened individual harbors an objective point of view on life, offering a broader outlook on all occurring events. A person guided by mutual respect and kindness rather than deceit and wickedness; someone without the intent to cause suffering to a fellow human being under any circumstances. Collectively, humanity needs to raise its level of consciousness and accept the truth; accept that we live in an imperfect world, but work together to build a future based on love and compassion. Earth, the home we were given, is being destroyed by man's way of life; its resources exploited for the concept of money, even though those resources are essential to the survival of mankind. Humanity must realize we have a greater purpose in the universe than simply being a species meant to grow wise, die and later face extinction.

Most importantly, the concept of enlightenment can be neither a religion nor a cult. No person can consider themselves in a position of authority because all souls are created equal. Each one must develop a genuine faith that stem from their own point of view, a personal relationship with the Universe. The awareness must arise from deep within, expanding as the mind interconnects various events of its personal life to spiritual wisdom. One's soul is unique, only the mind it is connected to is capable of conscientiously analyzing how spiritual truths are related to those events. Being Enlightened does not require anyone to let go of previous religious beliefs, provided that hatred, deceit or violence is not promoted in any way. Churches, mosques or other places of worship from religious institutions are still relevant due to all the positive energy they contain, and any form of prayer is simply showing respect towards the Universe, no matter the name it is given. An enlightened being still requires a strong personal faith.

A collection of spiritual truths and knowledge regarding our existence is contained within these pages. Words are important but their significance have limitations and can easily differ from one language to another. Therefore, while acknowledging what is written, also examine the broader notion or idea attached to the words' significance rather than which words were used or the way it has been written. Skepticism is only rational, but common sense, critical thinking and an open mind can link these spiritual concepts to any situation someone may experience on a daily basis. Reaching a higher level of consciousness takes time and effort, it will not happen overnight, and it certainly can not be attained solely by reading on the subject.

All branches of fundamental science have already revealed clues and decoded some aspects of our origins, but there is still much more to discover. Nonetheless, it might be difficult to find any tangible evidence to prove the existence of an ethereal realm. Yet, human senses, along with some use of common sense, may at times unveil the truth. For centuries, thousands of people have reported strange paranormal phenomenons all across the globe. It seems statistically impossible and irrational to discredit every single encounter as fictitious. With the idea that everything is energy and all energy is connected, it becomes conceivable for paranormal phenomenons to be a form of energy that we simply do not understand yet. Besides, scientists have already theorized about the possible existence of multiple dimensions or parallel universes. We can choose to dismiss what we have not experienced or do not understand, but it would be an oversight to reject unconventional ideas without a proper analysis. Even with prior beliefs, it is feasible to keep an open mind and stay receptive to new information. The universe goes far beyond what is logical to the human brain. Doubt must make way to faith. A soul can not evolve if it is guided by fear. If one lacks faith in life or the Universe, there can be no evolution of consciousness. It would mean the rejection of one's own existence. One may know yet lack the belief, but one must always believe in order to truly know.

What really defines us as an evolved species is our morality and empathy towards one another. We connect and relate to each other by sharing our creativity. We can understand how emotions feel and we have the capacity to recognize which actions or decisions could cause suffering to others. There is a certain comprehension that whatever happens, there are repercussions of some sort, that there is a cause to an effect. Yet, we have grown hateful and deceitful towards our own kind. Despite knowing that mankind sprung from a single source, the world remains oblivious of the bigger picture connecting us all. Humanity must learn to coexist in spite of all differences and accept what is unfamiliar rather than discriminate against one another.

Everyone is linked, our souls have been sharing this world since the beginning of its creation. We have reincarnated for many lifetimes, but each time looking and thinking differently. Even though it is possible for souls to cross path again in divergent lives, each body is confronted by a new environment and has a distinct thought process. Past cultures and civilizations are relevant to today's way of life because the people of the past are also the souls reincarnated today. We are collectively accountable for the injustices of this world. Humankind began sabotaging itself long ago, and now, the planet from which we depend on to survive is being affected by our choices. Increasingly, we have damaged Earth's soil, destroyed her natural resources and polluted the air we need to breathe, slowly accelerating the decline of human civilization. All are responsible for the survival of humanity, yet we allowed a few to benefit from the exploitation and devastation of our planet. We have accepted the illusion of power and the concept of an inequitable money system.

The world is in need of a shift of consciousness, where its citizens can respect and embrace the diversity of cultures and religions as well as the creativity emerging from all across the globe rather than spread hatred, ignorance and judgment.

The journey to Enlightenment begins when the conscious bears a will to access the information stored within the soul. With the help of meditation, a vital part of spirituality, the mind will develop a profound connection to the origin of our existence and bring forth an improved understanding of life. Eventually, the conscious will recognize how the soul, the body and the mind's energy interact with each other. In time, the consciousness will shift to a higher spirit; a being which has complete trust in its instinct and is in utter control of its behaviors and emotions. But self-development requires time for introspection and profound thinking for the heart to heal and the conscious to mature. By conducting an open minded and extensive analysis of the self, from daily behaviors, to intentions, to past incidents, and so on, the mind will begin to perceive how everything is related to spiritual truths. Still, to evolve the individual must dare to step out of the comfort zone and challenge previous ideologies on what life is and how it should be. Little by little, faith will establish itself, liberating the consciousness from fear or doubt about its origin, the universe and its purpose. To be enlightened is to be free.

II.

THE UNIVERSE

In the beginning there was nothing. Then, in an instant, the Universe came into being. It was neither male nor female, but it was the first energy to ever be. The whole of existence, everything that can be felt or experienced, derives from this single energy source. The Universe is omnipotent, part of every atom and particle, we live in it and it surrounds us.

Within the corporeal realm, there exist several forms of energy collectively assembling a perfectly balanced universe. Contrary to the types of energy created by mankind, all natural energies on Earth possess a polarity or an opposition which ultimately complements the other, causing the balance of both sides, such as the Earth's magnetic fields. For centuries, Asian cultures have carried this fundamental principle giving it the name of Yin and Yang. The Universe is also an energy and, therefore, has no gender. Yet, it is still subjected to the concept of Yin and Yang. In the tangible world, a body will be host to a soul of either masculine or feminine energy. Whichever polarity is the most powerful within the corporeal realm will ultimately influence which essence is predominant within the Universe itself. Currently of a masculine polarity, our Universe's balance will, at a certain point, flip to become of a feminine polarity.

There shall never be an energy source as potent and powerful as the Universe. In all realms, the energy produced by Love is the purest and strongest. The Universe's very essence is Love. It's energy is immaterial, but humanity, over time, personified it because it was easier for the mind to understand. Whether he is called God, Allah, or Holy Spirit is irrelevant; we all exist because of this original loving energy. Its multiple names are simply how past civilizations and societies have identified him throughout history in relation to their cultures, upbringing or personal ideologies. Technically, we are all talking about the same creator, the only difference is our understanding of who and what it really is. Religion is a man-made concept manufactured by our longing to understand the origins of life. Rather than worship or glorify one religion over another, humanity should simply acknowledge that a greater being does exists regardless of how other cultures have chosen to honor it. For centuries, the worshiping of religions resulted in so many conflicts and loss of lives solely because of disagreements over which belief was correct. Yet, every religious rivalry was, and still is, ultimately in vain considering the true message behind the scriptures – a message of love, kindness and compassion towards one another. What matters the most above all else is to be able to distinguish what is right from what is wrong, to appreciate and respect differences rather than cause suffering. The Universe's existence is not dependent on beliefs, even those who choose to live without a faith are still bound to live within this reality. No matter who or what you worship, Love will bring you closer to the Universe.

Considering our souls were created from its energy, the Universe can feel, perceive and experience everything happening in a person's life. Consequently, it will always know the true intentions behind someone's actions. If there is a wish to harm someone or to act a certain way hoping to further one's own path at the expense of another, the Universe will have that knowledge. On the other hand, it will also be aware of a person's remorse or desire to make amends for previous actions. No one can fool the Universe or hide their true intentions; its essence is far greater and more powerful than any soul it has brought into existence.

We all share a personal relationship with the Universe, but we can choose to reach out everyday, on occasion or when in despair. In fact, in times of need, most have often, knowingly or not, asked for assistance from the divine in the form of words, thoughts or emotions, such as wanting something considered important or for things to just work out as wished. When consciously seeking answers or spiritual guidance, prayer is often the most common and practiced form of communication; yet, the most effective and beneficial way is through meditation because it allows the soul to feel and experience its own energy as well as the Universe's energy. Despite the lack of an immediate response, it is always there and it always listens. Help from the spiritual realm will usually manifest in an unexpected way. The Universe will decide if, how and when help or guidance is provided. Much like a parent, it gives what is needed rather than what is wanted which is why its assistance often goes unnoticed.

With Enlightenment, it becomes easier to recognize how the Universe affects and guides our every day lives. When distressing events occur, it is easy to dwell in certain emotions or let despair take over. We are given challenging situations ultimately to try to learn from them. Keep in mind that the Universe is loving and will not put something on one's path unless there is a purpose. Though some situations may be difficult at the moment, something great can arise from their outcome. How these challenges are dealt with, however, depends solely on the strength and will of the individual. The Universe does not wish suffering upon us; yet as humans we would not be able to evolve if there were never any struggles. Through pain, we must learn and grow.

Creation

The Universe is and will always be the only being who truly knows and understands how the corporeal realm came to be. The absolute answers concerning our existence are far too complex for any human mind to grasp. Mankind, thanks to multiple breakthroughs in science, has already uncovered evidences contributing to the understanding of how life formed and evolved into what it is today. Modern theories such as the Big Bang and Darwin's theory of evolution have emerged and now seem to be the most compelling explanations for our world's creation. Nonetheless, the theory of a creator to all that exists, of a divine figure responsible for everything that is known, has traveled through time, cultures and civilizations, and is still prominent today. Yet, there is still much debate over which theory is correct. Evidence overwhelmingly suggests Earth was created millions of years ago; still, many mysteries persist over man's ancestry and the development of our consciousness. Realistically, for a consciousness to exist here on Earth, there is a need for a biological human body to have developed. Therefore, both creation and evolution could be legitimate.

Following Darwin's theory of evolution, the human mind was able to establish a logical explanation for nature's development. Still, there are multiple gaps of knowledge missing about the biological evolution of our ancestors to the modern humans of today. Archaeological remains may provide an insight into these changes, but will never be able to pinpoint exactly when the human race reached a level of consciousness with cognitive abilities capable of abstract thinking, innovations and sophisticated behaviors. Nor will they be able to provide understanding into how mankind possesses advanced moral values or why we are, in a sense, wired to experience complex feelings and emotions such as hope, faith and love. Human consciousness has always been far more complicated to comprehend than the evolution of our biology and genetics.

The real mystery of humanity's creation is not how life evolved, but when; when was the genesis of human consciousness. At what point in history were souls placed into human bodies to begin their evolution, to slowly start becoming aware of their existence, surroundings, thoughts and emotions. Ancient drawings may have been discovered in a cave dating to a certain age, yet it does not automatically signify that an entire species had a complex thought process at that approximate time period. Science can only do so much to try and understand our origins and can also only be right until new studies or discoveries reveal otherwise. Research is vital to our comprehension of humanity and the universe, there is no denying that, but it will not and can not entirely explain all of life's mysteries.

In scriptures, it is written that Earth and the cosmos were created in 6 days. However, the author's interpretation of his genesis vision should not be taken literally. In truth, the length of time from the Big Bang to the first human consciousness may have happened in a single instant from the Universe's perspective. What most individuals fail to recognize is that time itself is illusory; a man made concept needed in all aspects of life but with no exact measure or definite number. A young child before the growth of its cognitive abilities can only understand the "now", the simple fact that he or she is alive before being taught otherwise by our society. Most are unaware that the Gregorian calender, used today by western cultures, was only adopted in the late 1500's and was determined based on the records of ancient civilizations which did not have modern day technologies to measure time. Our solar system, and the entire universe, is ever changing; galaxies, stars and planets are always in movement and constantly affect the others. Which means there is always a possibility for our measurements or our calender to be revised once again. Our perception of time would be not be the same had humanity evolved on a different Earth-like planet. Nonetheless, the corporeal realm has a perpetual need for time and its various measures to allow us to properly function as an evolved species; and thus, the illusion persists. The Universe could have created the tangible realm at any point in time. Existence as a whole is infinite – it is this very instant and then the next. Neither life nor existence can go backwards; a human life may end, but the soul's existence does not.

Many theories and hypothesis have tried to make sense of how our cosmos was able to create the conditions necessary for an organism to thrive. Our reality seems fine-tuned so precisely that it is almost improbable for our universe to have materialized and evolved without a divine intervention. Could it really just be a coincidence? Sure, anyone can attribute life to a fortunate accident or luck, but the world can reveal a vast amount of evidences for our creation if we are willing to see them. There exists a perfection in certain shapes, patterns and even numbers which are manifested across all of nature, and there are hidden clues of our creation such as the similarities between the image of a brain cell and the universe itself which, thanks to the improvement of science, are now noticeable. Our evolution is far too peculiar to be attributed to something that just happened out of the blue; have faith in the Universe.

We have chosen to exclusively believe what can be perceived by the senses or explained by research and analysis. With science, there is a need for something to be observed and reproduced through experimentation before it can be accepted as factual, which is obviously incredibly important to our understanding of the reality we live in. The problem is that science can only explain how things function in the corporeal realm through natural causes. It may never be able to confirm the existence of the supernatural or to rationalize the abstract concepts of metaphysics.

The key to the understanding of life in the corporeal realm is within oneself – within the soul. Every consciousness is the creation of a greater energy. Enlightenment, the awareness of who and what you are, will ultimately reveal more about both life and existence than science or anybody could ever teach or explain. It is the only evidence there is to validate that mankind and all that is tangible, is the result of creation.

Religion

Mankind yearns for existential truths; we wonder about our origins, the purpose of life or what happens after death. This deep longing to understand such fundamental questions has lead to a search for answers and to the establishment of numerous organized religions. The concept of an all-knowing, greater being is part of our history. Archaeological and written records of ancient civilizations have shown that the human race worshiped divine beings prior to the appearance of any modern faiths and scriptures. In this day and age, organized religions have become so prominent that our schools are teaching children to accept the doctrines and ideologies of a belief system before they are able to form their own beliefs on what life or the world really is. How can a young child understand the teachings of an organization before it has the time to experience certain emotions such as love or grief?

Although religions have repeatedly been a source of conflicts around the globe, the root of these hostilities is not the belief in a higher being or its messages, but rather because opposite sides they are unwilling to accept the divergence in their dogmas and traditions. The inhabitants of this world appear to have forgotten that we are all descendants of the same ancestors, and ultimately, it is absolutely pointless to argue about who possesses the correct answer. Ancient texts and scriptures convey the Universe's messages of compassion and love regardless of the prophet who has spoken the words. These texts differ mostly within the particular laws and regulations that the adherent of the religion must follow in order to be a true believer. It does not matter what you wear, it does not matter how many times a day you pray and it does not matter which holiday you celebrate. Such rules are trivial matters of life written by a person, or persons, who have altered the texts to fit their own perspectives. The Universe did not write the scriptures, it only provided the messages. Perhaps the writers, along with anybody who may have rewritten and translated the scriptures, have added their own meanings to the messages that were initially received. Or, perhaps the messages were too abstract or profound to be completely understood.

Many have argued that religions are used as a tool to control the masses. It is somewhat difficult not to agree with this statement knowing that there are belief systems willingly chastising their followers if they do not comply to certain rules. Fear is constantly employed as a mean to keep the people obedient. Both Christianity and Islam, the two main religions of this world in terms of members, teaches that non-believers are automatically condemned to Hell. When using common sense however, one can argue about the naivety in holding a belief that a large portion of the population will unquestionably go to a place of suffering after their death solely due to the fact that they do not endorse one of these two faith. Still, when a person is tormented and concerned over an unknown future such as the afterlife, or when the person is being manipulated into a belief, it can be difficult not to fall prey to fear.

There exist so much hatred and bigotry in this world based solely on the writings of belief systems established hundreds of years ago. A single sentence, which has been translated and revised more than once throughout time, may today be the cause of animosity, torture or even death for someone who wants nothing more than to live peacefully. Homosexuality, for instance, is subjected to such discrimination even though there exists several records of same-sex relations in our history spanning across the globe and within many cultures prior to its consideration as a sinful act and prior to becoming a motive for persecution. Judging a fellow human being on the basis of a religious belief is harmful to the religion itself, causes greater suffering and is in direct conflict with the ethical and fundamental principle of being good to one another. The world has changed over time but the human race is still holding on to primitive behaviors. There comes a time when the population needs to evolve, to broaden its minds and awareness, to adapt to modern cultural developments instead of complying blindly to an old doctrine.

Nevertheless, not all organized belief systems are harmful or immoral just because they have, at times, been prone to antagonize the masses. In truth, the majority of people who have chosen or were nurtured into an organized religion have found their sense of purpose and are living virtuous and happy lives. No one can say worshiping a religion is wrong; on the contrary, it is a way of understanding the ultimate truth. Since we all have a unique relationship with the Universe, an individual's personal way of connecting with the ethereal can not be judged by others. We are all free to believe and pursue the religion or spiritual beliefs of our choosing. Keep in mind that each soul follows a particular path.

Today, faith in organized religions has been in a steady decline amongst the youth. Nonetheless, choosing to stay away from religious institutions does not signify a lack of faith. In truth, most adolescents are still going to ponder what life is all about; they only prefer to discover and learn on their own rather than be told via old doctrines. We each carry within us the ability to perceive what is fair and just from what is dishonest and unethical. Belief in religions may have decreased with time, yet there has been a substantial rise in spiritual values. Spirituality is a faith; the mind ultimately trusts and believe in its own insights and intuitive perception of the world. Every soul is free to pursue self-growth, to gain wisdom through experiences and to find its connection with the Universe on its own and when it is ready to do so. The extent of one's devotion towards a chosen faith is insignificant for the Universe does not demand glorification from its creation, but the acceptance of its existence.

There is no organized system affiliated with the expansion and awareness of one's own mind, and there are no specific establishments in which a person should worship the Universe. It is up to the individual itself to recognize and observe the laws by which our universe functions. The path towards an enlighten mind influences one's moral judgment and will serve as a guide when the time comes to make tough choices. An individual must learn and realize the significance of love and life on its own accord along with the only belongings it was given upon its arrival in this reality; a mind, a body and a soul.

III.

ENERGY

In spite of our knowledge on energy, the masses reject, doubt and remain unaware that many sources of metaphysical energies are part of our environment. For instance, mainstream science does not acknowledge the existence of paranormal phenomenon for there is no verified physical evidence. There is also doubt expressed over any mention of transcendental experiences, and despite the idea of karma being known globally, its legitimacy is still overlooked. Emotions like love or anger, which we are constantly releasing in our surroundings, are energies as well, generated and sensed by our spirits to communicate and relate to one another. The ethereal realm even contains beings capable of interacting with the energies in our reality. In truth, energy is the tie that binds the entirety of existence together.

One of the main laws in relation to the nature of energy states that it can neither be created nor destroyed. Instead, any form of energy is perpetually transformed into another form. The entirety of our Universe consists of energies, interconnected to create a balance, a whole, in all things. Amongst our reality, we know of multiple ways energy can transform. We are aware that some natural forces are interdependent on one another, such as the Earth and the moon. Some metaphysical energies also function with an opposite force. The spiritual principle of contrary but complementary powers demonstrates that certain energies, unlike those transformed from matter, are never fully black or white; the dominant polarity contains a fragment of the other. For instance, a soul of masculine predominance still possesses some aspect of femininity and vice versa. The combination of both is what creates a balanced soul.

This universal life force concealed within the mind is independent of our bodies. It bears its own kind of energy which has existed prior to birth and will continue to exist after death. In short, we are energy beings with an awareness confined to an organic vessel. Despite our souls being of the same origin, which is an energy greater than ourselves, every soul is unique just like all human DNA is unique. Physically, identical twins share the same traits even though, while their DNA may be similar, both have very distinct personalities. Of course, nurture is partly responsible for their difference but still, even as infants, their character differ.

Emotions are essential to the growth of our awareness as they are used daily to connect and interact with our peers. In this material realm, we are fortunate enough to be able to physically experience how uplifting love energy can feel. Unfortunately, fear and grief, in spite of being unpleasant, are just as fundamental to one's growth in life. A consciousness could acquire valuable insights from physical or emotional pain. We can relate and experience sympathy towards someone who's suffering because we're all familiar with the way it feels. Collectively, we share this knowledge and we know how the mind can be affected by those sentiments. We are aware and we understand that love can strengthen us and fear can cripple us. Any emotion, when felt intensely, could take over the mind and, consequently, trigger a profound change of perspective in one's beliefs, character or ethics.

Remaining in control when feeling overwhelmed by an emotional state of consciousness is a valuable ability to possess and develop. Emotions are contagious, for instance, anger has a tendency to spread around to the surrounding environment when expressed. Often, the recipient of that anger will start to feel similarly, also producing its own negative energy as a reaction. The way an emotional response is handled will have an impact on subsequent behaviors, and may lead to spontaneous actions that could potentially be damaging to our self, our personal destiny or karma. Controlling an emotion does not signify suppressing it, however.

It is still important to experience all emotional states for they may be a potential lesson to learn. But to show restraint when handling the negativity of others lowers the possibility of attracting negativity for oneself. There is always a transfer of energy happening, and with a strong will, even a single thought with harmful intentions will be projected out into the universe and towards the person it is intended to. We are confronted with the energies of others every day while trying to manage our own. The mind is a powerful weapon in a world filled with selfishness and hatred, let's attempt to be empathetic and kind to each other instead. Perhaps we can spread a bit more positivity in our surroundings.

Unconditional love will always be perceived positively. But some of the emotional states we experience can release energy from both edge of the spectrum, depending on the circumstances. The feeling of surprise, for instance can be experienced as both positive or negative. And, at times, there are moments when the challenges we are faced with have more of an ambiguous outcome. Life is a complex web of interacting energies collectively creating their own future as it unfolds. To keep the balance, the world can not only be black or be white, there are, and there must be, many grey areas. How the mind chooses to respond is influenced by many things. Mental illness, emotional distress, peer pressure, all could impact the way we deal with a situation.

Our soul functions in the same way as our corporeal body; both need to regenerate the energy that has been depleted. Sleep does not only allow us to regenerate our body after physical effort; but it also grants our soul the much needed rest and rejuvenation after interacting with the energies of the world. Just like the body, the soul also suffers from lack of sleep which consequently weakens its spiritual defenses. Sleeping however, is only one of the multiple ways a person can replenish their spiritual forces. Some of the best sources of spiritual energies are places of spiritual devotion, where people gather to practice their faith. Or, if one has a strong connection with nature, the soul has the potential to absorb the energies of the earth, so go where nature is still untouched. Vice versa, avoid places that are considered wicked, where evil has been allowed to enter or where malicious deeds have been carried out. Still, some locations are situated in the grey areas. For instance, a cemetery is considered sacred as well as corrupted. Nevertheless, meditation will always be the most direct and efficient way to reach and restore spiritual energy.

Energy surrounds us, whether generated artificially, naturally, or spiritually. Energy is energy and will always be energy no matter the source; it is existence itself. Understanding the different ways our spirits interacts with the world can broaden our horizons and bring us closer to the path of Enlightenment. Learn to become aware of the energies around you and teach your consciousness to control its emotions. When experiencing the emotion of love, bear in mind that it is the most powerful energy source in the universe.

Ethereal Realm

Our cosmos is merely a small portion of the whole of existence. Beyond what is seen lies a larger and more complex realm that is not perceptible by the five basic human senses. As energy beings, we were never meant to experience the entirety of creation through human senses alone. For instance, our ears are only capable of hearing frequencies inside of their limited range, still it does not mean that frequencies outside this range do not exist. Despite coexisting, we are unable to perceive the ethereal because both realm are not meant to interact directly. Acknowledged throughout time as the afterlife, the underworld or limbo, the metaphysical world is essentially everything that happens behind the curtain of our reality.

Metaphysical energies prevail at a different frequency than the corporeal cosmos, and therefore, are not bound to its laws of physics. The ethereal realm is home to innumerable energy beings and also contains an unknown amount of dimensions

— Heaven and Hell are such examples. Once a soul's greater purpose on Earth has been fulfilled, it travels back the immaterial universe where it will continue on the journey of its existence. Retaining memories of the afterlife while inhabiting the physical realm has the potential to interfere with the lesson that is meant to be learned. Instead, anterior knowledge of our existence is concealed deep within the mind's subconscious. The soul prompts the mind, via intuition, not to make the same errors it once made.

Because a soul in the ether is on a different plane of existence, it can still hold a distinguishable form and choose how it would like to be perceived. If a human being was to witness the metaphysical realm, it would observe a vast collection of entities and beings of all shapes, sizes, colors and appearances. What is experienced all depends on individual perception. A soul in the afterlife becomes completely self aware. While emotions can still be experienced, they do not have power over the spirit self. The non-corporeal realm seem like a utopia where all are oblivious and blissful. Love is the only emotion which can be expressed to the fullest as an energy being.

Some human beings may possess the capability to somehow interact with the unseen while others may only be able to catch glimpses, like the ability to perceive a person's aura. Mediums, psychics and others have already described supernatural experiences involving another world; it would be highly doubtful as well as statistically impossible for all claims to be fraudulent.

The Veil

With the intent to protect us from what our minds are not meant to see, a universal energy was put in place to act as a buffer between the realms. The veil of reality's primary function is to keep us from perceiving anything ethereal such as wandering spirits or entities. Vice versa, it also prevents non corporeal beings from interacting with our world. Yet, there will always be exceptions. Which is why some people catch glimpses of what is considered supernatural. As a second function, the veil's energy counters our desire to constantly seek a higher perspective on life and prevents us from deviating from our current destiny. The veil will distract the mind, and on occasions modify memories and mindsets, as soon as the path you are meant to travel is in danger of being altered.

The veil's effectiveness fluctuates depending on the mind's level of awareness. Children for instance, are more prone to breach the veil because they are oblivious to the reality of the world around them. Most are unaware of the struggles of life; they have no bills to pay, no responsibilities to uphold and no past to dwell on. Likewise, the veil's grasp is less powerful as we reach old age due to the mind becoming weaker and vulnerable. Children and elderly alike are more susceptible to experience the supernatural, yet, both are dismissed by adults because their minds are busy dealing with managing their daily lives and keeping up with their adult responsibilities. The more preoccupied our minds are, the stronger the veil's influence becomes.

Throughout history, there are reports of individuals capable of seeing beyond the veil. Traditionally, these people are given an important role in their community. They use their gift and serve their neighborhoods as shamans, seers, mediums, psychics or spiritual guides. Some are born with their abilities, others gradually learned to peek through the veil. In certain circumstances, one can obtain such a skill involuntarily due to traumatic events that the mind can not deal with, or due to someone trying to cause you harm through magical means. Regardless of how one is able to pierce through the veil, you have the choice to embrace it or to ignore it. True fortitude is required to handle what is hidden by the veil; one must consider it has a gift rather than a curse. If you choose to embrace it, be benevolent and help those around you.

For those seeking the enlightened path, it is important to remain aware of the veil's grip as it will attempt to suppress the spiritual self. For instance, while one attempts to meditate, the veil's energy may cause distractions to keep the mind occupied elsewhere. Knowing how the energy of the veil operates can aid in remaining consciously aware of its interferences. As one slowly becomes enlightened, the path may begin to seem like a lonely road due to the veil trying to keep anyone who is spiritually aware away from those who are not. Yet, sometimes, solitude brings introspection, and that is when a person truly starts to see their life under a different lens. Isolation could help achieve personal growth and may lead away from harmful behaviors or habits.

Since the beginning, we have biologically evolved alongside the fauna and the flora of Earth. Our mind's evolution has surpassed all other living creatures, yet certain species of animals, such as canines and felines, seem capable of sensing or seeing what we are unable to. Some have a heightened awareness and can foresee danger, others appear able to perceive what is on the other side of the veil. The reason may simply be that they lack self-awareness and therefore, they are of little consequence to the veil. In certain periods of history, ancient Egypt for instance, felines were considered sacred because of their alleged ability to protect and ward off evil spirits. The Wiccan community renewed and broadened the belief that any small animals, not just felines, can serve as guardians from the spirit world. The term *familiar* is given by practitioners to the creature chosen as a personal protector from the wicked. Having a pet is not only beneficial to one's life, but it will also aid and enhance one's spiritual journey.

Thus, this protective cloak ultimately preserve the balance of harmony and chaos between both realms. Remember that as humans, we are not meant to see or handle what the veil covers. Without its energy, our minds would be unable to cope and process the sight of metaphysical beings and multiple dimensions all at once. There would be no way to distinguish what is in our reality and what is not. Some souls have successfully been able to break the veil's grasp in their lifetime, but whether that event is fortunate or unfortunate depends on the individual's own perspective. There exists a way to reach this ability, but be warned, once the veil has been lifted, it can not be undone. Those who do so, must do so at their own risks.

IV.

ENTITIES

Humans are not the only conscious beings amongst the realms of existence. The Universe also created greater energy beings meant to preserve the integrity of the grand design. These entities are given a specific purpose to help them accomplish this task. The strongest of these beings are often referred to as Angels; they are the ones who have stood by the Universe's side the longest.

At the time of its creation, an entity lacks the freedom to choose and is driven only by the will to fulfill its purpose. Yet, as there is always an exception to the rule, it is possible for an entity to obtain the ability to decide for itself. Also, depending on the given responsibilities, some entities are allowed to exist in both the physical and metaphysical realm.

The Universe doesn't just give existence to an entity if there is no need for one. There must still be a balance in all energies roaming our realm. The Yin/Yang principle applies to all energy beings; thus, there are those meant to do good and others meant to do evil. Angels may be the greatest entities fighting for the righteous, yet many other entities considered to be on a lower level are just as important. Likewise, the influence evil beings can have on the corporeal realm varies depending on their purpose. Stronger entities can have direct repercussions on human lives, such as Death. The entity of Death however, is misunderstood because despite taking life away, it is neither good nor bad but rather neutral. It is devoted to its task of keeping the balance of energy here on Earth.

Still, many entities are not designed to interact with human souls but, instead will impact the environment. A virtuous entity will protect the Earth and influence its elements; their duty is to preserve nature. At times, an entire region may be in peril due to human activities or pollution. The entity charged with its oversight will interact with the ecosystem in an attempt to repair the damage. A hostile entity will instead affect the surroundings in a negative way. For instance by spreading diseases, impeding the growth of the flora or disturbing the natural evolution of the fauna.

Entities by default are not able to feel any emotion. Therefore, if tasked with proliferating a certain emotion, the entity may have a desire to understand what that emotion feels like. In order to do that, the entity must inhabit the corporeal realm through a corporeal vessel. By doing so, it will gain a new perspective and understand how humanity experiences that emotion. The vessel however, usually remains unaware of its situation, living its life normally to ensure the purity of the emotion. If sharing an existence with, let's say, the entity of Love, the love felt in the individual's life will be magnified and the entity will project that emotion back to the world. The stronger the love felt by the individual, the stronger the love felt worldwide. On the flip side, if the person lacks love in its life, the weaker it becomes around the world.

There are other circumstances that can make a corporeal vessel suitable for an entity to occupy. Someone, for instance, could be the victim of an incident resulting in a coma or a near death experience. The person's soul might cross over to the ethereal realm, leaving an empty vessel behind for another being to take its place. Truth is, a corporeal body does not need a soul to exist because any human being will still have a personality, retain memories and live a standard life. If an entity was to replace a soul, it could impact the person's original behaviors and personality. Evidently, these events do not always result in an entity inhabiting the physical body either. But to allow themselves some leeway to accomplish their tasks, entities will purposely let a number of people grow older without a soul. These physical hosts are specifically created as additional resources in case an event does not unfold as planned. In fact, if needed by the bigger picture, any soul can be reincarnated in a host that is already a grown adult and still be completely oblivious of their condition because they would still have recollection of their time growing up as children.

Some entities are too powerful to exist in the corporeal realm due to the importance of their role in the grand design. Many of which have found their way into our ideologies such as destiny, karma and fate.

Destiny

Whether aware of it or not, all souls pursue their own independent path forged in time by Destiny. The entity of destiny resides exclusively in the ethereal realm because it is charged with forging and overseeing every single potential path. Unbound by time, Destiny operates alongside Fate and Karma, amongst others, to guide the entirety of the corporeal universe into what it is meant to become.

There are infinite paths a soul can take, especially due to the gift of free will that we each possess. If an individual's will changes its destiny, there is potential for the ripples to affect other people's path. Yet, Destiny is a stronger energy being than humankind, it has the ability to counter the effects free will create.

Despite constant changes in people's destinies, we remain oblivious to those changes because the veil will disguise them. In reality, an event, an action, an encounter, anything really, can prompt modifications in one's future. With our busy daily lives, we must always make decisions; therefore, there could be an infinite amount of possibilities. As we are unaware of our purpose, what may seem like luck or coincidence could in fact be a change towards the intended path.

One's free will could cause changes in a person's destiny that are irreversible. If a person, for instance, is meant to be an athlete but instead breaks a limb due to their free will, they would be unable to pursue that path. In this case, Destiny must design a new path while taking into consideration any ripples that were left behind. As an example of the ramification a change in one's destiny may bring, let's pretend that the athlete in the previous example was meant to inspire a child. This child will now never be inspired at the right moment in time to point him towards his intended future. With the child's own future in jeopardy, it carries the potential to create ripples of its own, damaging more destinies in the process. The entity must step in and find a new way to inspire the child and ultimately guide him back to the path that was originally predestined for him.

We must always be mindful; a decision on a trivial matter may in fact be life altering. When uncertain, let the soul be a moral compass. If listening closely when in need of guidance, it will point towards a path that will feel right. Even though we do not know what our purpose is, our destiny is always tied to the destiny of others. Individuals in a position where they have the ability to affect destinies on a large scale due to their power or influence will be held at a higher accountability by Destiny.

Reaching enlightenment can also alter what is pre written. Before becoming an enlightened being, one must reach a higher level of spirituality where it is able to understand and accept the Universe's grand design. The mind acquires wisdom and with it a new desire to be part of a greater purpose. It is likely the original path can no longer be followed due to one's new perception of the world. In this case, Destiny will forge another path where the individual's role in the grand design will be more proactive. Yet, when enlightened, a soul's destiny will remain fluid and the Universe will position it wherever needed most.

Fate

Fate is not just a synonym of destiny; it is a separate entity that operates alongside but independently from Destiny. Even though the latter is a stronger energy, Fate possesses greater abilities. Humanity as a whole must also follow a path, because we are not only evolving as individuals but also as a collective. The human race has a collective future which results from certain events that are inevitable yet necessary. The entity of Fate is in charge of those events; it has the ability to overwrite anything that could threaten the future of humanity.

The world has gone through many major changes in the last two millenniums alone. Events causing a significant impact on a global scale are likely to be the catalyst of a long lasting effect on mankind. Psychics and prophets of the past have written to warn us about what they foresaw in the future, but fate is still unavoidable as it is improbable to accurately pinpoint the catalyst of such events.

As an example of what could be a fated event, and presuming World War II was part of the grand design, take into consideration the story of the British soldier who spared Hitler's life during World War I. It was said, by Hitler himself, that during his time in the German army, he encountered a soldier on the battlefield who had the opportunity to kill him but never did. In this scenario, Fate may have had to intervene to preserve what we now know as our past. His death was postponed because he was fated to play a bigger part of our history. Even though he ended up rising to power, once his purpose was fulfilled, he met his demise.

Fate may seem inescapable, but a being with tremendous willpower and freewill can change its fate, despite unknowingly changing the supposed course of events. If one is ever able to change fate, than the entity would find a way to achieve the Universe's goal in a different way, but the result can potentially be worse than originally intended.

Karma

The layout of our daily lives is all part of destiny but what is put on our path is mostly determined by karma, the universal force influencing the future based on our integrity. Karma, as an entity, strives to maintain the balance of give and take.

The idea of Karma's retributions is one of many spiritual notions that has been embedded into various cultures for generations. In fact, it is one of the few cosmic truths that is still alive in our modern world.

Unlike the two previous entities, Karma's work is perpetual, meaning there is so much to do that it requires the entity to be fully immersed into the purpose it was given. Its task is also far more complex because it accounts for all the soul's lifetimes. In the beginning of a soul's existence, its karmic balance is zero, neither positive nor negative. However at the start of its very first lifetime, destiny must forge its path. Some will end up fortunate from the start and others will not, but unfortunate circumstances should never be used to justify a poor moral judgment. In the entity's eyes, everyone is judged the same no matter the person's ethnicity, culture, religion or how it identifies. We must think of the moral consequences to our actions. If our intent is to do a good deed out of kindness, than good karma will be awarded, and vice versa.

Karma's role is also to make sure that everyone is accountable for their actions. A person's intentions are the only unit of measure by which the entity determines what side effect will ensue. If an action has led to something negative and it was not the intent, Karma considers it. However, an act of selfishness compels Karma to settle the karmic debt and generally, the rule of three is applied to determine the appropriate repercussions. For instance, if one takes something unjustly, karma will invoke the rule of three and take something of equal or up to three times the value of what was taken. Likewise, if you were the unfortunate party, you will be given something in return. Nevertheless, know that one's karma can be paid back in any of the soul's lifetimes, do not despair if you feel that justice has not been served.

The cosmic balance of our universe: positive versus negative, good versus evil, is maintained in part by Karma. To do so, it requires the help of Destiny because the consequences of an individual's bad karma can create ripples and affect another. The effects of Karma however are infinitely complex; when bad karma is being paid back, the outcome may not necessarily be an eye for an eye. Most of the entity's reprisal are overlooked by the individual because of his unawareness of karmic justice, but also due to the veil protecting karma's work.

As human beings, we must recognize that what we decide to do will have consequences and we should consider how our actions ultimately impact not only our personal path, but also the life of another person. We must show compassion and act selflessly because what we have can be taken away just as easily as it was given to us. Understanding the mechanics of Karma is a step towards an enlightened path.

Karmic parasites

Many beings and entities that roam the realms have the ability to divert a soul's karmic energy towards themselves. Just like a parasite, these individuals can sustain their good fortune by leeching off of their victim. The person afflicted by the parasite is not necessarily aware of its condition, besides a string of what appears as simple bad luck, there are no indications that it is under psychic attack. Only a strong spiritual soul would be capable of warding off a parasite or reducing its damage without seeking help. But one can minimize the risk of affliction by staying away from places such as where the dead rest or where evil things have occurred in the past. To further shield ourselves from harmful intent it is always wise to wear protective tokens or enter a holy place or a place of worship. If the affected soul does not free itself from the parasite, it could damage the soul or threaten its destiny.

Karmic balance

When progressing towards enlightenment, karma is called upon to settle one's karmic debt to the universe and will begin adjusting its karmic energy in the direction of the positive spectrum. Due to a greater knowledge and awareness of the universe, a being on the path of enlightenment will be held at a higher karmic accountability and its life will start to segue to a new purpose. Karma must now settle the debt but it can not risk disrupting the path by simply causing one major event that could provoke a negative impact on the soul. Therefore, the debt is never settled all at once, but over time. Facing its karmic dues is a mean for the soul to gain wisdom. Even if poor moral decisions were made in the past, any future repercussion should be seen as a learning experience. Nevertheless, paying back negative karma is not a pleasant ordeal. A true selfless act of kindness will go a long way towards paying back a karmic debt.

As mentioned before, Karma is a complex entity. There is in fact, more than one karmic account corresponding to one's existence. Each lifetime, has its unique karmic balance as well. For instance, if Destiny gives a privileged and fortunate start in life to a person, chances are some dark times can emerge in this person's future. On the other hand, if a person's past is troublesome, it does not mean that the tide will not turn in its favor later in life.

The perfect lifetime does not exist here on Earth; good fortune and difficult times are not everlasting. Nonetheless, Karma's role is not to take away the good fortune it has given, but one must give back when possible and with the intent to do good. As humans, we must not allow greed, envy or pride to influence our judgment; showing compassion and aiding a fellow human being is the essence of positive karmic energy.

By understanding how the cosmic cause and effect functions, a person has the means to maintain a good karmic level. Karma continuously strives to keep the balance of give and take which may at times look like the world is against you, but know that nothing lasts forever, neither good nor bad times. Gratitude for what we already have and generosity towards the less fortunate will improve our chances at a good life in the eyes of Karma. Greediness and malicious intent are the quickest route to losing everything.

V.

SOULS

Each of us is unequivocally a unique being. Nevertheless, a given name, a genetic body and a singularly developed personality nurtured by its background is not a person's authentic self. One's soul is the subconscious instinct that we have when we suddenly feel insecure about something happening in our lives or when we get the desire to create a change due to an unhealthy lifestyle. Everybody's true self has existed prior to this life and their universal knowledge lays dormant within us until awakened. Some of the answers to existence are hiding there, all there is left to do is reach to the energy deep within and access its insights.

The Universe is the only energy able to bring a being into existence. If another could, the universal balance of energy would risk falling into anarchy and becoming unstable. Following its creation, it is essential for a soul to begin its journey within the cycle of life. The entity of destiny must determine where to integrate this new being and construct its path. The Tree of Life then transitions the soul from the ether into the body it will inhabit in the corporeal realm. Souls do not get forged at random, each must have a specific purpose in the grand design to accomplish at some point during their existence. A being's true purpose can be fulfilled in any lifetime, or while it travels around the ether.

Initially, the Universe brings us into existence as a whole entity, as both male and female energies that are unified. But the entity must then be separated into two essences, masculine and feminine who will search and yearn for their other half while in the physical world. Still, whether a spirit is of male or female energy does not automatically signify that it will also be its physical gender in the corporeal realm because ultimately, souls have no control over the body they will be born in. Depending on the needs of the grand design, a masculine spirit can potentially be born in a woman's body. Likewise, a feminine spirit could be in a man's body. It is even conceivable for both souls to be born as the same gender. This notion alone can rationalize how two people of the same sex can love one another or how certain people feel that they were born in the wrong gender. If a person is gay, lesbian, bisexual, transexual or experiences any gender related dysphoria, the reason may lie with their own being.

Fundamentally, we are part of the Universe's grand design as conscious beings meant to learn and gain knowledge about our existence throughout our journey inside the cycle of life. With each new life, a new chance to become a better being. A soul's essence is altered by everything it experiences, therefore, one's past lives have influenced its present, and will have influence in the next life and so on. At one point, there will come a time when the soul will evolve to reach a more profound and abstract level of understanding about existence. All beings must experience the teachings of life, so that all beings can prepare for coexistence.

More than a singular lifetime is needed for a soul to grow wiser. A life without an end would hinder one's growth and would defeat the purpose of learning from previous mistakes. Every life is a clean slate, a new path where the soul acts as the compass guiding the mind through the journey it experiences. Reincarnation is necessary so that everyone is allowed the same chance at redemption, if needed. When there are no more lessons to master and no more purpose to fulfill, the cycle of life ends and the consciousness is ready to cross over to the afterlife. The amount of lives a soul must live to end the cycle of reincarnation varies for each being. All souls evolve at their own pace; some will experience less and some will experience more. It is dependent on multiple factors including one's karmic debt or the time spent with its other half. Still, even if one has reached the afterlife, it is not impossible for the grand design to require the soul for a different purpose at a subsequent moment during its existence.

We all share this world as individuals who must find a way to coexist. Today, people find themselves persecuted simply because they do not fit in or are increasingly subjected to prejudice because of their appearances. Whether a person has a physical or mental disability, a different skin tone or the opposite gender is irrelevant because we are not our physical bodies. Each and every one of us has a past and a story that deserves to be heard as much as anyone else's. The mind who is accepting of all regardless of appearances or divergences in terms of lifestyle, religion or even opinion has already taken a step towards the enlightened path.

Soulmates & Cosmic Companions

Throughout a lifetime, a person can experience a number of connections to certain people that will feel more profound than other interactions. As souls, we continuously yearn to find our other half, the perfect match to our energy, and it is possible to spend some time with them in the physical world.

When the Universe splits a being in half to become two separate souls, also known as soulmates, both essences enter the cycle of life independently and apart from each other. It is in their destinies to unite again in the corporeal realm, but only when both are ready and have settled their karmic debt. In truth, soulmates only cross each others' path sporadically; not in every single lifetime. They must first be able to control their energies while being in proximity of each other. If soulmates were to encounter before they were meant to, they would risk being overwhelmed by their immediate chemistry and would slowly start withdrawing themselves from the rest of the world. Both would be consumed by their love and would abandon their occupations, their ambitions or even their lifelong dreams, basically destroying their destinies in the current lifetime.

When soulmates come across each other's path for the first few times, they usually do not get to be in close proximity for very long. For instance, it would be two strangers waiting for the same bus or smiling at each other in an airport. Over the course of lifetimes, they will increasingly happen upon one another until both successfully learn how to handle the emotional energy of love. Only then, depending on their personal growth and their ability to manage each other's presence, will both halves be allowed to live together as soulmates.

While we relentlessly search for the person meant for us, we also interact with many other souls over the course of our multiple lifetimes. Every time we interact with someone new, we voluntarily agree to exchange energy with them, instantly creating a sort of cosmic bond between both. This energy connection can either be positive or negative and as the relationship develops, the bond becomes greater. Our souls are capable of recognizing these profound connections. As a result, when it remembers a companion or someone important from its past, it transmits the emotion it is experiencing to the mind. Such as the impression of already knowing someone recently met, or even a sensation to just stay away from them.

An indefinite number of souls exist in this realm and the possibilities are endless for who we cross paths with, when, and in which life. We also sustain old bonds and create new ones with any relative, close friend, love interest, or person significant enough to influence our lives. Entities like Destiny and Karma make souls travel as clusters to better keep track of everyone. These clusters are also used because it is easier for two people to grow as beings when there is a profound connection between both. When around a cosmic companion, our souls tend to behave similarly to how they did in the past to encourage us to learn from our mistakes. Thus, when we share our experiences, exchange knowledge and learn from another's perspective, we also benefit from each other and aid in fulfilling our place in the grand design.

All clusters are interconnected, being part of one does not limit any soul from ever interacting and developing a cosmic connection with someone in a separate cluster. There may come a time however, when two companions have learned all they could from one another and will cease to cross paths in future lifetimes. In some instances, a cosmic link can also be broken if two people have come in conflict with each other, if one prevents the other from growing any further, or if one has become too emotionally attached. The latter circumstance becomes a problem if it is time for the other soul to reunite with its soulmate.

Broken Souls & Broken Destinies

Despite being given a purpose and a predestined path, there are souls whose cycle of life will be interrupted, either due to the freewill of others, or because they have experienced something emotionally traumatic enough to damage their core self. If a soul breaks, it loses its connection to the Universe and can no longer continue on its intended path or fulfill its purpose in the grand design. The suffering is usually so great that a broken soul will bear its injury over multiple lifetimes in hopes of finding a way to heal itself and reconnect to the Universe. In the process, however, it could also jeopardize the paths of many by transmitting its negative energies. Which is why ultimately, if the psyche is unsuccessful in its quest to recover, it will be removed from the corporeal realm and continue its existence solely in the afterlife.

Sadly, as we navigate through the unpredictabilities of this world, a single event that is distressing enough can disrupt one's journey through life if the mind does not manage to overcome the trauma. As children or teenagers, when unable to survive on our own, we are at our most vulnerable, and susceptible to the will of others. Even as adults, we may, at some point, be the victim of circumstances and suffer from physical or psychological trauma capable of breaking our spiritual selves. Still, there are occasions where a series of bad decisions slowly amounts to a disrupted life cycle. A person who continuously takes the wrong roads will damage their own future in the process. If the entirety of their good karma ends up drained, negative energy will begin to accumulate instead, and carry itself over to subsequent lifetimes. After a while, unless the individual finds a way to heal spiritually, the soul will give up on hope and, eventually, break. One's downfall can also be caused by gradually letting oneself be controlled by its vices, be corrupted by others with malicious intent, or by deliberately walking the sinister paths of life. Harming another being intentionally will deplete a soul of its spiritual energy and of its connection to the Universe, changing the course of its path in the grand design.

Every so often, a person could be exposed to some damage that will not break the soul itself but only the destiny it was meant to follow. Unlike broken souls, a broken destiny will not affect the soul's energy or its attachment to the Universe. When its life ends, it will be reborn with a new path and the cycle of life will begin again. Nonetheless, its karma is still being accredited. In comparison, a broken soul, on a day to day basis, is unable to find love and true happiness and perpetually wonders how to repair itself. A broken destiny instead, drifts through its life without motivation, constantly searching for something to aspire to. Typically, one's path is shattered either due to circumstances involving other beings, or because the soul itself has damaged the intended destiny by making the wrong choices. The entity of destiny withholds from forging a new path if the soul purposely refuses to pursue the one initially given. Similarly, if a soul such as a wandering spirit somehow finds a way to a body meant to be a corporeal host, it could be reborn without a predestined path. Like broken destinies, these pathless souls experience their lives feeling unfulfilled and yearning for a sense of purpose to fill their void, unknowingly awaiting the next cycle.

The main priority in the existence of souls that are either broken or without a path is to find a way to repair the damage and find a raison d'être. A broken being's energy is weaker due to its lack of connection to the universal energies; therefore, psychologically, it is more prone to misbehave. By doing so however, the person could compromise the soul and destiny of other people in its surroundings. As an attempt to regain its strength, a broken individual can divert the spiritual energies of others towards itself, effectively using their energy for its personal benefit. If enough spiritual energy is misappropriated, then the other person's destiny is also threatened. One must always be cautious when allowing someone new access to their personal life. Since a person voluntarily chooses to share a bond with another, it exposes itself to the will and intention of the other, so establishing mutual trust first is surely worthwhile. Occasionally, if two broken beings find each other, they could become mutually dependent and neglect their pursuit to recovery.

A damaged person will unconsciously seek anything or anyone potentially beneficial for its recovery. Yet, broken or not, the soul alone has the power to mend itself. One's own will to confront the past, cope with the torment and let go of its burden can provide the necessary strength to overcome this dark chapter in its existence. If successful in its journey towards health, the newly restored soul can reenter the cycle of life and regain a purpose. As individuals, we can only help and guide a broken being if we are aware of the cause of its suffering. We must remind ourselves to stay vigilant yet sympathetic as we may at some point also be in need of hope.

Past Lives

Mankind has always been accountable for its own history. Thanks to reincarnation, we've essentially been our own ancestors since the beginning. In fact, it is important to understand that even with a constant population growth, new souls are not being created every time a baby is born. In reality, the vast majority of souls alive today have lived more than a single life already; therefore, being an *old* soul is much more common than presumed. Although, quantifying the lifetimes one has gone through is insignificant if the soul itself has not grown into a wiser being throughout those lives. In our world, an old soul is only recognizable if the individual actually possesses a greater awareness and appears to be more mature and intuitive than others.

The existence of a soul is not bound to time in the corporeal universe; therefore, it is not necessarily reborn in a linear manner. Which means that despite currently living in the 21st century, our next lifetime could very well be in a previous century. The entities writing our paths and guiding us to our purpose are in charge of determining where in time we need to be reborn. It is unlikely, albeit not impossible, for a soul to have two distinct lifetimes during the same time frame. Although, both lives would need to be secluded from the other, because we are not intended to come in direct contact with a past or future self.

A human mind would be unable to cope with all the knowledge acquired from a considerable amount of lives and therefore, when a soul inhabits the corporeal universe, its memory from all previous lifetimes are suppressed. Yet, even if we are not meant to remember when we've lived, who we were, or what we've accomplished, some souls may be able to catch glimpses of their past, either during meditation or due to something triggering a memory in their mind. Still, depending on the consciousness, remembering the past may place someone in a precarious position. Occasionally, if the moment being recalled was a distressing experience for the soul, the individual would become increasingly preoccupied which, in turn, could develop into an irrational fear. Others with recollection of a former vice must be cautious not to relive the past and let it sneak back into their current lifetime otherwise there is a risk to repeat the same errors as their previous selves. The present should be the focus as there is more wisdom to obtain. Furthermore, a being can also deviate from its current destiny if the memories were to become too vivid. The soul would start to withdraw itself from reality and the mind would experience confusion and delusions.

Although, to have some recollection of a past life can also be regarded as a great opportunity. At times, a glimpse can be a direct message from the soul to the mind, a way to communicate something of importance. Some introspection is often necessary to analyze the message and understand its significance. If the mind is strong enough to ensure it will not hinder its growth, exploring a memory and reflecting on its influence on the current life could be beneficial for the soul's progress in the cycle of life. If a connection between the past and the present can be established, a choice must be made between moving on from the history of a former life or risk being undermined by it.

A soul can be reborn again and again trying not to repeat the same error as a former self. A person is not wiser based on the number of lifetimes it has experienced. It is an individual's ability to understand the teachings of life which truly matters in the grand design. The Universe has conceived all of us with the means necessary to process whatever we are faced with no matter how harrowing it seems. Being able to self-analyze and introspect on the past or even on the current lifetime is valuable. Improving oneself sooner rather than later will undoubtedly shorten the time spent in the cycle of life.

Free Will

The freedom to choose is imperative and plays a major role in the grand design. Without our ability to make a choice, the balance of power between good and evil would be prone to point towards the positive side. In reality, even if a soul's destiny is pre-written, it must choose to be a righteous and compassionate human being of its own free will. One has to come to its own conclusion between what is right and what is wrong. The power of one's will is imperative to resist being tempted by the reprehensible. Despite the awareness that every choice will bear future repercussions, anyone can still voluntarily walk the wicked path. The decision to remain virtuous serves as a test of strength for the soul.

Free will is a gift humanity is fortunate to possess. Many entities in the ethereal realm do not have the luxury to choose, but are instead designed for a different purpose. These entities seek a specific objective and follow a designated course of events. For instance, an angel is inherently holy and can not simply decide to commit a malevolent act, unless it is part of its fate to do so. Throughout its existence, an entity can also earn its freedom to choose by somehow demonstrating its eternal loyalty for the greater good above all else. Even a recently deceased spirit with enough willpower can decide to stay in the physical realm for whichever reason. Any being can be created with, or earn the right to decide; nevertheless, nothing is as vile and disgraceful as one who uses its will to cause pain and misery.

Even if guided by a destiny, the soul can only communicate its insights with the mind in subtle ways such as a thought, a feeling, an intuition or a mental image. Thus, the human mind—along with its memories, its behaviors, its unique reasoning and its tendency to be influenced by emotions—possesses the ultimate power to choose. As individuals, it is important to remain mindful of the feelings transmitted by our soul before making a choice to avoid acting impulsively. Despite any circumstances, there is always a conscientious choice to be made. Alas, the outcome can not be controlled by the soul nor the mind; whatever the ramifications are, they are part of life's uncertainty.

If ever under the impression of not being given a choice and that the results seems unfavorable, one must choose what is right despite the consequences. And if ever instructed to commit an appalling act by someone with the illusion of power, one must use their free will and make the arduous decision of doing what is honorable rather than what is instructed. It is time to assume full responsibilities for the choices that we make regardless of the situation because at the end of the day, they will affect the course of our current and future lives. Those in power who are aware of or complicit in immoral deeds being done, are just as accountable for the impact they cause despite not physically participating. It is essential to understand how powerful free will can be and utilize it to make the world a better place to live in.

No matter what, we must do our best to not let others influence our decisions. Humanity has long suffered at the hands of those who use their will to cause anguish. If we allow certain people to get away with injustices because they are in a position of authority, we inadvertently contribute to the illusion of power that they hold over us. Moreover, we collectively need to exercise our will to insure the survival of future generations and preserve the resources provided by our planet. Let's not forget that we are all here because of the will of the Universe.

The Afterlife

The ethereal realm is composed of multiple dimensions within its infinite space. Generally, a soul who has accomplished everything it was meant to while in the cycle of life will be ready to travel to a higher plane of existence. Once there, it will continue to exist in either one of the two dimensions commonly known by mankind as Heaven and Hell. Still, one can reach the afterlife despite not having fulfilled all of its purposes. Indeed, a broken soul who interferes with the grand design will be removed from the physical world to continue its journey in whichever dimension it belongs in. A being who is evil in nature and commits unforgivable deeds against humanity and the Universe is taken out of the cycle to prevent further damage to other people's path and is likely to spend the rest of its existence in Hell. Vice versa, a being who has lived righteously and has opted for love and kindness throughout its journey in the material realm is likely to rest in Heaven alongside its soulmate.

On occasions, it is possible for an individual who has engaged in a path of deceit and suffering to be guided by a pre-written destiny. In reality, not every being who has committed a despicable act is automatically condemned to spend the rest of its existence in everlasting torment. If written in one's path to cause physical or psychological harm to others, it may be because the soul has a greater purpose to fulfill, or a specific lesson to learn. For instance, a person who behaved recklessly may need to learn how it feels to be remorseful. There are times when we must experience something to fully understand its implications. It is the totality of our actions during the cycle of life that ultimately determines our destination in the ether.

Certain entities, like Karma, are involved in the passage of a soul from the corporeal realm to the afterlife dimension in which it belongs in. However, there are many alternatives attainable for a soul in the continuation of its existence. Every now and then, some spirits will be allowed to explore the intangible realm or even be given a new task to accomplish in the cycle of life. Moreover, some may be granted a new purpose to either guide someone towards its destiny or protect another to secure its future. The Universe may also reward a virtuous being with the opportunity to transcend into a higher being and ascend to the next level of understanding. Unfortunately, it is possible for certain souls to be incapable of crossing over to the intangible realm; in which case they will wander around aimlessly in our world until they find a way to reach the other side.

Heaven & Hell

Most faiths of the world have described their idea of Heaven and Hell as paradise being a place for the righteous and the underworld being for the wicked. Although it is fairly accurate, the cycle of life as a whole must be taken into consideration when one is ready to reach the afterlife. A singular life is simply not enough to assess the true nature of a being. What influences the outcome is not related to who a person was or what its societal beliefs were. The true factors which will determine where a soul is headed once it reaches the afterlife are its behaviors as well as the intent behind its actions. Thus, chances are that an individual with a decent moral judgment who usually does not aim to cause harm to others will continue its journey towards the bright side. Those who are purposely vile will not be as fortunate.

A dimension is essentially an ethereal universe, similar to our corporeal realm, and can be just as vast in terms of proportion; meaning that there is more than just one area or place to go to within it. For instance, both Heaven and Hell have a central location; a permanent nexus of energy. Souls are also restricted to a region that is separate from where entities are able to interact with others. As each individual soul will evolve with distinct ambitions and desires, one's perception of what is heavenly is undoubtedly not the same for everyone, and one's punishment in Hell must somewhat be related to the atrocities it has committed. Therefore, souls have their own little pocket of corporeal universe in the afterlife, to either experience whatever they wish or as part of their reckoning. In other terms, there isn't just one Heaven and one Hell; there is one for every soul.

When one attains paradise, it is basically granted its own private domain in the dimension where it can manifest anything it wishes for, and pursue the rest of its existence however it chooses. If wholeheartedly desired, a soul can experience the beauty of corporeal life again but this time, without any uncertainty since it creates its own future. A soul who reaches Heaven may also seek to spend the rest of its existence harmoniously alongside its soulmate in a shared perspective. One could prefer to interact with other souls also in the afterlife and maintain the various energy connections it has established while in the corporeal world. Regardless of how one desires to experience the afterlife, there is always a possibility to continue growing as an energy and acquire more awareness about existence and its bigger picture.

Contrarily to those headed for the virtuous side, the souls en route to Hell will not be given the freedom to decide what is next for themselves. Since the dimension is designed as a punishment for committing terrible deeds, the retribution should correspond to what is deemed worse from the soul's own perspective. Much like in Heaven, each soul is given its own personal Hell. However, not every soul who has arrived there will be condemned to eternal torment. Indeed, some soul may only have terrible karma to redeem; in which case the soul's occupancy in Hell will be short-term. Others may need to experience the atrocities they have inflicted onto others. Eventually, if the soul is able to atone for its past crimes or learn whatever it is meant to, it will be allowed to return to the cycle of life and given another chance at existence. A being who willingly creates suffering in the world and chooses to disconnect itself from the Universe's energy or its grand design will surely be in Hell for the long haul.

In actuality, by nature we all belong somewhere. Whether good, evil, or in the grey zones, the Universe still has a purpose for all of us.

Near-death Experiences

A soul's energy begins its transfer towards the ethereal realm at the brink of its demise or shortly after the body took its last breath. Nonetheless, even if the soul has already departed, a person could potentially regain consciousness if the circumstances are in its favor. Occasionally, someone who experiences a near-death event may be able to preserve the awareness of everything it perceived during its travel through the ether. As each possesses a singular perspective, those who cross to the other side and return will detail their experience differently; some may recount how it felt and some may talk about what they observed, while others may describe an encounter with another being.

The cause and resulting impact of a near-death experience are also unique for each individual. In the grand scheme of things, surviving death could be written in one's path, be caused by someone else who deviated from their own path, or even due to a personal decision which wasn't part of one's destiny. Depending on the situation, the soul might require assistance from a guiding spirit to return to its physical state. This spirit will manifest as whomever will make the soul feel at peace during its time between realms. Upon its return, one's consciousness is likely to be altered by whatever it has experienced. At times, the effect can trigger an epiphany which prompts the individual to significantly change the course of their life. On rare occasions, entities may be compelled to radically deviate someone's future to cater to the needs of the bigger picture. Fate, for example, has the power to substitute the soul of an individual who's gone to the afterlife for another soul or being. The original soul is either reborn or in the afterlife while the body continues to live normally despite its new resident.

VI.

THE SUPERNATURAL

Usually, most people get curious if a conversation on esoteric or paranormal topics arise. Although, many still lack belief and may be quick to dismiss or even mock the idea that supernatural phenomenons are part of our reality. In fact, anything related to the ethereal realm could be considered supernatural, including religious practices as they suggest the existence of otherworldly elements. Various aspects of the spirit world are entangled with our own; all involve ethereal energies. Whether it is through eerie manifestations, clairvoyance abilities, divination techniques or by employing magical means, thousands of people already encounter or engage in activities involving the supernatural every day.

Not everyone is intended to have faith in a religion or the spirit world. Oftentimes, those who are not receptive to supernatural energies that surround them are likely to never encounter something out of the ordinary during their lives. Therefore, they will remain skeptical because they have not experienced anything on a personal level. On the other hand, a number of individuals are more susceptible to perceive and interact with the metaphysical forces of the ethereal realm. In any culture, there are people who have either developed or acquired the ability to look beyond the veil of reality to discern spiritual energies. A seer, for example, can foresee what is to come from a broad perspective. Nostradamus notoriously sought or received visions about the world's future even though he did not necessarily comprehend what he saw.

Due to the uncertainty of our world, many may seek guidance or answers in relation to their past, present or future. Psychics and mediums are among those capable of using their own senses and intuition as instruments of clairvoyance; although, each has distinct methods to achieve their goal. Generally, a psychic will focus on getting specific information from an individual's path by seeing or sensing the energy in their environment such as one's aura—a unique and forever changing energy signature bound to a person's emotional and psychological state. A medium functions in a similar fashion; however, they are also proficient at establishing a direct channel between the non-corporeal realm and ours. They are usually able to feel, hear, see and at times communicate with the deceased or any other spirit willing to open a dialogue.

In certain cultures of the past, unnatural phenomenons were often misunderstood by the majority and characterized as demonic or as a product of witchcraft. Witches were thought to be responsible for such occurrences and condemned as practitioners of evil who used magical means for personal gain. Today, even though the term magic is frequently regarded as preposterous, it does not make its subsistence any less legitimate. In essence, magic can be defined as the manipulation or influence one can have over the spiritual energies of this world. Depending on the intent of the practitioners, magic can either be beneficial or cause harm. A shaman is known to employ the energies of the spirit world to heal and help others in their community, while dishonorable practioners will control the energies for darker purposes.

Yet, because the Universe and ethereal entities strive to maintain the universal balance of all energies, practicing magic can entail consequences. Manipulating universal energy as mere entertainment is a risk for it can disrupt the balance even if the individual does not intend to. In such cases, any repercussions are tallied up on the individual's karmic debt. To discourage people from upsetting the cosmic balance, all successful energy manipulation operates on a three-fold law. So, whether the spiritual forces are influenced for good or malicious intent, the effect will return to the sender multiplied by three.

As energy can only be transformed, when a person employs magic to impair another, it uses the essence of its own soul to call upon a wicked being lingering around in our realm. Basically, a wandering spirit is given a purpose to interfere with the life of the individual targeted. Depending on the intent, the effect of a magical spell can impact the physical, mental, emotional or spiritual state of the victim. Likewise, the same principle applies if witchcraft is used for one's good fortune. Except this time, the spirit called upon will strive for the well-being of its target. Nevertheless, not every bewitchment will involve a non-corporeal being. Occasionally, ill will from a magic practitioner can be directly transmitted to the intended victim if both know each other personally. One should avoid sharing personal objects with, and refrain from accepting drinks or meals from an untrustworthy individual.

Magic should be used solely with pure intent and mainly to defend and protect oneself or loved ones. Traditionally, burning sage or frankincense is known to cleanse negative energy and keep evil beings at bay from an area; although, the effects are only temporary. Wearing a special charm or any religious or spiritual symbol of choice is also advantageous for one's protection. Nevertheless, only true faith renders a charm powerful and effective.

Universal Messages

Beyond our realm, the Universe, the entities and the many beings in existence are continually communicating and interacting with one another. In our world, despite being concealed by the veil, these divine dialogues are being heard, intercepted or consciously received by spiritual and non-spiritual people alike. A few have also noticed recurring patterns in the cosmos, which have resulted in certain fortune-telling methods like numerology, palmistry and astrology.

Universal messages are frequent; in fact, quite a few are hiding in plain sight and intended for the whole of humanity rather than a single person. Within the history of mankind, many parallels can be drawn between events that have repeated themselves throughout time, despite different eras, cultures and circumstances. Because each soul has its own perception of reality, a message that is noticed can be interpreted in many ways. Perhaps the consciousness believes it is a warning sign for what is coming; or alternatively, a signal for the world to act before it is too late. Keep in mind; there is a purpose for everything.

Along with the information being transmitted to non corporeal beings, universal messages may also be exclusively intended for and perceived by a singular individual. A sign meant specifically for one person is often repetitive, such as meaningful coincidences or a recurring number in the span of a few days. Even though the actual significance may not be completely understood, communications from the beyond are directly relevant to one's life and aim to guide the soul on its journey. Further methods of correspondence may also be experienced through vivid dreams, visions and spiritual manifestations. The mind attempts to decode the sign as it personifies everything seen, heard or felt. An objective look at the timing, the message's details and anything that relates to the individual may suffice to determine its importance.

Fundamentally, the cosmos is comprised of patterns, sequences and elements which are necessary to the grand design. Across time and cultures, people have discovered some of these hidden codes while attempting to predict their future or when requesting spiritual assistance. In the modern world, multiple clairvoyance and divination techniques are known to establish a direct link with ethereal energies. However, one should still remain cautious in the pursuit of counsel from the beyond because certain methods are not suitable to all. The Ouija board and tarot cards for example, might entail consequences and should be practiced only by strong spiritual individuals. The board is known to open an immediate channel with a spirit that is called upon. However, its response is unreliable as the spirit who actually answers the call is rarely the one sought. Whereas, the tarot card approach may not require immediate communication with a spirit, but it still seeks answers from any spirit who is willing to respond, whether righteous or wicked. If one of these two methods are to be used inside a home, consider cleansing the area, as well as anyone around, before and after the practice because a spirit can linger inside a room and attach itself to any person accessible. Alternatives like horoscopy, ancient runes or the I-Ching are safer for they do not involve a direct link to an otherworldly spirit.

Anyone in pursuit of spiritual guidance is capable of doing so by themselves since all it requires is the user's own conviction for divination to function adequately; although certain methods may necessitate years to learn and completely hone the craft. Nonetheless, the answers obtained might be ambiguous regardless of the chosen technique. Oftentimes, due to the constraint of a decoding practice, the response is up for interpretation. The individual must attempt to relate the message to their personal life and contemplate its significance to effectively comprehend its relevance. It is recommended to seek universal advice from a form of divination that one feels comfortable using. With time, it will become easier to understand and make sense of the answers. Still, solicit ethereal advice solely when important and appropriate.

Furthermore, any person could inquire about their own personal future from universal codes simply by asking the proper questions. Various individuals may also be born with an innate ability to interact with ethereal energies, either by sensing when an event is about to transpire or by predicting events before they happen. The problem with clairvoyance and prophesies is that all the choices we are faced with on a daily basis are constantly changing our personal destiny as well as mankind's collective future. Plus, if necessary for grand design, nothing could stop the Universe and its entities from altering the original plan. Merely knowing too much information about what is to come elevates the risks of modifying the path, and there's no guarantee that the alternative won't be worse. Countless variables are susceptible of changing the timeline which is why some predictions wind up unfulfilled.

A broken soul with the will to heal could possibly intercept information circulating in the ether. For a few of them, divine transmissions will emerge as a subconscious thought – a phrase or a single word with the potential to inspire and restore hope in their future. The message often become words to live by for the individual – an anchor keeping the mind focused on its task to recover.

Meditation

A person's inner self is the most efficient and powerful resource available to reach out to the ethereal realm and explore the wonders of existence. A soul already bears a direct energy connection with the Universe; establishing contact with the immaterial only requires a relaxed body and a mind focused on its innermost self. Through meditation and with great will, Buddha was able to merge his conscious mind with his subconscious, accessing the knowledge of his deeper self and finding the answers he sought. Many forms of meditation are known to achieve a higher state of consciousness. In fact, to tune the mind to universal transmissions is the ultimate tool and fastest approach to acquiring spiritual growth. Any meditation practice can be mastered over time with persistence, perseverance and an open mind. Still, it is important to choose a method which allows the consciousness to focus and rid itself of worries and distractions; some may prefer a technique which includes movement while others may simply wish to reflect in a stationary position.

Prior to meditation, it is mandatory to find a quiet place to unwind and avoid being interrupted. Additional elements could contribute as well to attaining a meditative state, such as cleansing the area of negative energy, blocking outdoor noises with headphones, or even listening to calming melodies. While attempting to concentrate exclusively on the moment, it is often effective to direct one's awareness on the breath. It may also help to envision the self in a setting that feels peaceful and secure–a personal space, whether imaginary or not, where the mind is free to go anywhere. For new practitioners, it may be a challenge to let go of trivial thoughts during the first few sessions. Eventually, with sufficient practice and patience, the soul will wander and take the spirit on a metaphysical journey. Let the self be guided by the adventure as it may lead to where is needed, and trust the inner voice as it may convey messages of wisdom and virtue.

Once a spiritual link is created, the soul has the freedom to undertake whatever it desires and there is a wide range of possibilities. A person may devote its time to the exploration of its own existence whereas another could yearn to find peace of mind and spirit. Another could aspire to hear the messages broadcasted by the ether, or even interact with entities and beings. If the purpose of meditation is to experiment with spiritual energy, the individual is able to do so as well. Nonetheless, some of those ventures exhaust the energy from a soul's essence more than others. As a simple way to replenish the spirit, regeneration is practiced by visualizing the self somehow absorbing, or connecting with, the Universe's energy.

Each mind will experience mindfulness from a singular viewpoint. The universe does not communicate with words that can be heard through human ears. Instead, transmissions are subtle and arises directly from the consciousness' thoughts and imagery. Thus, the journey is perceive by the mind as it sees fit, and can invoke from personal experiences to help understand the messages's intent with more clarity. A person's intuitions and its emotional response to the meditative state are key elements to consider when trying to comprehend a message's significance. Avoid self doubt and allow the mind to go anywhere it needs to.

The veil strives to obstruct and limit one's spiritual awareness from causing damage to its personal destiny, unless it is time for the soul to walk a different path. Practicing mindful meditation can teach oneself to control its emotions and impulses.

If enlightenment is desired, frequent meditation is a prerequisite to keep in touch with the spirit self and the Universe. Neglecting the path for long periods of time is assured to diminish a person's spirituality. Rising to an enlightened state of mind will require time and discipline.

VII.

GREATER PURPOSE

Fundamentally, life in the corporeal universe is a parallel for existence as an ethereal being. Humankind's inner nature strives to find happiness and to live in peace despite the hardships of life. In the ethereal realm, there may not be physical or mental torment, yet every energy being – virtuous and vicious alike – still seeks to exist amongst others. Coexistence for all its energy creations is the Universe's ultimate purpose. As a piece of the grand design, the role of the human race is to seek spiritual knowledge so every being can understand how we all relate in spite of physical, cultural, theological and ideological differences.

Whether mankind will achieve cohabitation on Earth remains unknown. However, acknowledging our reality's ethereal truths would undoubtedly bring about more love, compassion and acceptance to the world – which is a good place to start.

Every single energy consciousness in either realm is a unique and important component for the Universe's ultimate goal of coexistence. In fact, a few universal principles are essential for the grand design to operate freely, and are relied upon to eventually attain this greater purpose. The law of cause and effect, for instance, substantiates how everything and everyone is interconnected and can be affected by one another. Hence the necessity for entities like Destiny to give an alternate path to anyone whose journey in the corporeal realm has been significantly impacted by another person. The disruption of a person's destined course within the cycle of life hinders the soul's energy transformation, possibly jeopardizing its role in the grand design in the process. Unfortunately, there will always be nefarious beings with the intent to corrupt and wreak chaos in another's existence. So, the grand design is also rigged with a fail-safe: the universal truth that, in the end, good would always triumph over evil. After all, for both polarity to coexist, the whole of existence must settle at the perfect equilibrium of energies.

While in the corporeal cosmos, everyone experiences their existence from an individual mindset–the adventure is completely subjective. However, to progress and thrive, the human race needs to unite as a collective force and strive to improve the quality of life for all current and future human beings. The world ought to realize what is truly valuable in life and shift its consciousness to create positive change. Regardless of societal or economical status, everyone has a personal purpose to carry out, and all abide by the same universal principles. All souls are, at their core, forged on the same groundwork as any of their peers. Thus, no one is of greater importance for the sake of coexistence.

Human souls were always intended to be flawed creations. The concepts of power, greed and hatred were embedded into humanity's inner nature as temptations that all must confront independently. Throughout lifetimes, each being must choose to overcome these subconscious weaknesses rather than yield to them. Temptations are specifically designed to be appealing, and the possibilities are infinite for what could be enticing to an individual. Oftentimes, wicked beings will seek to corrupt souls by exploiting these vulnerabilities in hopes of disrupting the universal balance in their favor. To resist being tempted when faced with the notions of power, greed or hatred tend to suggest that a person already bears a good moral judgment and is well on its way to becoming a loving energy source.

To be in control or to have influence over the behavior of others, or over the course of events, does not always lead to wrongdoing simply because it is one of mankind's underlying flaws. Whether or not a person voluntarily chooses to put their own self or their desires before the welfare of others is governed by ethical motives. Righteousness can be harvested from a position of power if handled with a sense of responsibility, while taking our planet and the people's well-being into consideration. Still, the feeling of power does bear an increasing and relentless longing for more; humility is one's best shield against its grasp.

Similarly, the notion of greed involves an excessive yearning for something, often of material and superficial nature, that can only procure a false or temporary sense of happiness. In general, greedy behaviors stem from selfish purposes and personal benefits, such as manipulating a situation or taking what belongs to another. Though the combination of both power and greed could prove far more damaging to both the individual and the people affected by its avarice. To share what is of excess can bring much more value to life than to stockpile what is of trivial importance. Along with willpower, temperance and appreciation of what is already in one's possession are key to reject self-centered desires.

Sadly, a soul devoid of power or greed could still fall prey to its inner human nature. Ignorance, fear and discomfort towards the unknown or the unorthodox is known to fuel prejudice and discrimination, creating division and discord around the world. Whatever is considered different can be cause for hatred—race, religious beliefs, culture, way of life, even a divergence of opinion. As the polar opposite of love, hate is an energy nearly as powerful and overwhelming. It is up to each individual to overcome the hatred within them. At heart, all humans are the same, it is essential to choose empathy and sympathy over antipathy and ill-will. Through knowledge and love, weaknesses of the soul can be conquered.

Coexistence in the corporeal realm can only be attained if the human race subsists; and regrettably, in the last few centuries, we have increasingly sabotaged our own survival. Entire species of the fauna and flora are being eradicated while earth's resources are being exploited and polluted because a few are being allowed to destroy it for profit. While many have already taken up the cause to save the planet, they can not efficiently repair the damages unless everyone work collectively to put an end to its devastation. Living in harmony with nature should be a fundamental ideal, for it is our only home.

Ultimately, whichever the realm, all beings in existence ought to accept the omnipresent diversity. One's consciousness has to stay cognizant of the grand design and perceive the world from an unbiased and open mind. For mankind to coexist, every person has to progress and find solutions to mutual problems.

Path To Enlightenment

Each individual's journey to spiritual enlightenment is a personal one. Everyone must choose to accept the truths of existence independently, and at their own pace. Many souls may not be ready to increase their awareness to ethereal truths yet, and will not progress toward the path of enlightenment until a subsequent lifetime. Others who already hold a curiosity about their inner selves or the meaning of life, and those who have stumbled upon spirituality throughout their lives, are more likely to acknowledge the Universe and elevate their level of consciousness. Still, the complete acceptance of existence's true nature generally does not happen over a single meditation, as it did for Buddha. Enlightenment is typically a long process which requires exertion, self-discipline and most of all: faith.

To trust that there is existence after life, and to recognize that there is a supreme being, is essential to grow into an enlightened soul. Though, a person also ought to believe in its personal insights, during meditation for instance. Otherwise, any headway toward spiritual answers would come to a halt due to a lack of serious intentions. A soul can only convey its wisdom via the mind through imagery, and via sensory perception including intuition. Therefore, one must rely upon a strong faith in its own spiritual awareness—in what is felt and experienced. Everyone perceives the universe differently; being open-minded to the possibilities is of utmost importance. Doubt only brings about pessimism.

Only the pure-hearted can attain enlightenment; primarily because the wicked and the corrupt's behaviors are in direct opposition with the intrinsic nature of being enlightened. Those who are conscious of the consequences of their actions, but still reject spirituality because of a lack of belief, are simply less likely to evolve during their current lifetime. However, fundamentally, a soul's awareness to universal principles develops with each new life, and eventually, the circumstances will be suitable for the soul to transcend to a new state of consciousness.

To walk the path of enlightenment does not signify that one will automatically begin to live a utopian life. Karma may still have a debt to settle, and the outcome of any future situation could yield an ambiguous choice between what is right and what is wrong. In such a context, an individual should rely on their knowledge of universal principles, and should remain attentive to the guidance of their soul. Regardless of the resulting effect, the intent behind the decision is the main factor considered for any eventual karmic retribution. The reality is, no one will ever live an entire lifetime completely free from misfortune, suffering or obstacles.

In fact, hardship, sorrow, grief – all are necessary for the evolution of a soul and its understanding of the grand design. Emotional intelligence – to be capable of recognizing, managing and expressing an emotional state of being – is a considerable advantage while on the journey to ethereal knowledge. The mind has to confront its emotions rather than finding ways to avoid or suppress the feelings. Furthermore, instead of letting their behavior and thought-process be influenced by their state of mind, a person ought to find a way to control, express and/or release the emotional energies it experiences by whichever means. If what is needed to let go of negative emotions is to cry, listen to music or talk to someone trusted, then do so. As long as the emotional state is liberated in a harmless way regarding oneself or others.

An enlightened perspective on life typically causes distressing events of the past to resurface as the mind will be inclined to reflect on what has happened, and will attempt to relate the situation to spiritual concepts. However, to continue further on the path, the consciousness is required to address the incidents that still impacts the pursuit of its growth. In due time, the soul will seek to heal, and wish to liberate itself from all negative consequences provoked by those events. The objective is to unburden oneself of deep-rooted obstacles to be able to proceed on a brand new path with peace of mind. It may take a great deal of determination to reminisce on a painful past and recognize how it has affected us; but, it also takes a greater deal of inner strength to stop feeling angry or resentful about what is history, or, depending on the circumstances, toward one's own self. Forgiveness is the answer.

Nevertheless, what may be impairing a person's spiritual development is not always related to past occurrences. Occasionally, a soul's progression can also be hindered by negative aspects of it's lifestyle, such as a destructive behavior, a personal addiction or an unhealthy relationship with another person. If that is the case, one ought to find a way to remove the element keeping the soul away from happiness and general well-being. To acknowledge what the issue could be, it may be beneficial to solicit professional help, or ask the point of view of someone considered trustworthy for support and guidance. Supposing a person is incapable of parting ways with whatever impedes its soul, its spiritual development will simply be halted from reaching a higher state of consciousness. Nonetheless, the mind will still carry the knowledge of what it has learned, so the individual can return to its pre-destined path and experience life from a different perspective. Maybe one day, everything will become clearer and the soul will successfully evolve to an enlightened being.

Enlightenment is only attained when both mind and soul are merged perfectly, meaning the individual experiences everything with a constant awareness of the universe and its fundamental principles. A being that is enlightened understands the ethereal laws of the world and can live righteously, in coexistence amongst other beings. The mind is in control of its emotional impulses while the soul prevails over its egotistical temptations. Although, to maintain self-awareness and faith in the universe's design could prove challenging. At times, specifically during a period of trials and tribulation, one's thoughts could quickly be overwhelmed by the feeling of uncertainty. In spite of whatever happens, stay on the path and carry on making ethical decisions with love and compassion.

Generation of Enlightenment

The world is in a dire need of change. For the past centuries, mankind has been held hostage to a system of oppression, inequality and injustice. Those in power have favored personal interests and material possessions over the well-being and prosperity of the population. Corporations were given consent to deplete and contaminate the Earth of its natural resources in spite of knowing that it would aggravate the effects of climate change. Meanwhile, global conflicts and warfare are to blame for ages of unrest and grief. Nevertheless, sooner or later, change is inevitable. Humanity itself holds the power to revolutionize the state of the world in which it exists. Although, it is up to all of us to decide whether the future that is currently being created will be harmonious or chaotic. The time has come to learn from the past and thrive for a better tomorrow. Cohabitation on this planet is an achievable goal if every nation is intent on purging the world from poverty, corruption and hostilities regardless of borders.

Humankind will recover from dark times, as it has before in its history. But it is our responsibility to build a world where wisdom prevails. Keeping things as they are because of the convenience, rather than adapting to recent circumstances, is causing negative repercussions on a worldwide scale. Humanity ought to abandon what is outdated and adjust how it sustains itself, especially if it is aware that the current way of doing things affects the health and welfare of future generations. Because of our complacency and the unwillingness to create change, challenges are already on the horizon. Only as a collective will the population overcome what the future holds.

People ought to free their minds from the grasp of this materialistic and egotistical world. Independently, there must be a choice to look at life under a different light and to see through the veil of consumerism and capitalism. Trivialities of the corporeal realm are not essential to one's existence; and therefore, can only provide a temporary sense of happiness. It is mentally that inner peace must be found. Only then will the journey through the cycle of life seem effortless, despite whichever obstacles and temptations one might experience. A person equipped with spiritual wisdom and love at heart will find stability in its life, and see the beauty in both humanity and the whole of existence.

A generation of enlightenment is about to dawn on the human race. An age of progress where knowledge and conscientiousness pave the way to an equitable and understanding society. A world where all cultures are valued, where acceptance overcomes judgment and where ignorance makes way to tolerance. A place of hope, love and kindness where people have empathy for each other. A new era of our evolution where human minds are open to the possibility of an unseen realm. A time when humanity is not afraid of its future, and when the earth is finally respected. A generation which will innovate and uncover solutions to the mysteries of our realm. This future will transpire when love is chosen over hate, hope over despair, wisdom over ignorance, and faith over doubt.